Nicola Jackson

Difficult Women

Indigo Dreams Publishing

First Edition: Difficult Women
First published in Great Britain in 2018 by:
Indigo Dreams Publishing
24, Forest Houses
Cookworthy Moor
Halwill
Beaworthy
Devon
EX21 5UU

www.indigodreams.co.uk

Nicola Jackson has asserted her right under the Copyright, Designs and Patents Act 1988 to be identified as the author of this work.
© 2018 Nicola Jackson
2nd edition January 2019

ISBN 978-1-910834-88-6

British Library Cataloguing in Publication Data. A CIP record for this book can be obtained from the British Library.

This book is sold subject to the condition that it shall not, by way of trade or otherwise, be lent, re-sold, hired out, or otherwise circulated without the author's and publisher's prior consent in any form of binding or cover other than that in which it is published and without a similar condition including this condition being imposed on the subsequent purchaser.

Designed and typeset in Palatino Linotype by Indigo Dreams.
Cover design by Ronnie Goodyer.
Printed and bound in Great Britain by 4edge Ltd.
Papers used by Indigo Dreams are recyclable products made from wood grown in sustainable forests following the guidance of the Forest Stewardship Council.

To Roland, steadfast supporter and feminist,
and our sons Adam, James and Oliver,
with all my love.

Acknowledgements

Many of these poems were written as part of my MA in Writing Poetry awarded by Newcastle University and the Poetry School, London in 2017. I am grateful to my tutors Clare Pollard and Tamar Yoseloff for their insights and advice, and to my student friends for their thoughtful encouragement.

Thanks go to the editors of the *Morning Star, Carillon Magazine, London Progressive Journal,* the Hippocrates Prize 2016 (for which I was commended) and *Write To Be Counted* (2017) where some of the poems have already been featured. Much of the historical work is based on Robert Harborough Sherard's report *The white slaves of England, being true pictures of certain social conditions in the Kingdom of England in the year 1897.* I salute the extraordinary women he describes. Several poems have origins in the *Dreamers Awake* exhibition in 2017 at the White Cube, Bermondsey, and the final line of my poem *America* is a quote from Jonathan Jones in the Guardian Online 2017.

I was absolutely delighted that this collection was a winner of the Geoff Stevens Memorial Prize 2017, awarded by my publishers Indigo Dreams. Dawn Bauling and Ronnie Goodyer have provided endless encouragement, kindness and enthusiasm and have worked tirelessly to produce this collection. I am deeply grateful to them.

Lastly I would like to offer heartfelt appreciation to all my friends and family who have encouraged me in this venture, and in particular to Roland who has believed in my abilities from the start and lived with this book with patience and enthusiasm over many months. Thank you.

Also by Nicola Jackson:

Write to be Counted, Poetry to Uphold Human Rights, Eds. Jacci Bulman, Nicola Jackson and Kathleen Jones, (Cumbria: The Book Mill, 2017).

CONTENTS

Hinterland	9
How It Is	10
Chainmakers: The Long Cry	11
Chainmakers: Hephaestus	12
Chainmakers: Breaking Chains	13
Cradley Manifesto	14
Emily	15
Connie Markievicz	16
A Binding	17
I put my cup on that high shelf	18
Nest Egg	19
Wolves	20
Saturday Morning	21
My Sister's Bones	22
Lycanthrope	23
My Blue Tattoo	24
Searching the Lost	25
Stocks	26
My Mistress Masters All	27
Choice	28
Zebra Longwing	30
Walk in the Wood	31
Part Speech	32
Tooth Fairy	33
Le Grand Art de ne Pas Tout Dire	34
Skywatching in Yosemite	36
America	37
My Wall	38
Washington Seashore	39

Newcastle Down	40
Zazel attempts to become the first human cannonball	41
On Shingle Beach	42
Night-time in Brexit	43
Burns Night	44
Blood	45
Woke	46
Blue Bed Women	48
White Bed Women	49
Eidólons	50
Siren Sewn	51
The Place at the Other Side	52

Difficult Women

Hinterland

I summon scraps from the earth.
I tear tinfoil with my teeth.
I have handed all control

to one who is not aware
of where I am. She inhabits
a dimmed room where metal

threatens, where I am not heard.
Where my wish shouts down a tunnel
where I fear I will disappear.

You are a rasp inside my pubis.
You are an unaskable question.
My currency is bankrupt –

the Land of Nodding Dogs.
My muscles tear. I tear at myself.
I fear your heart beat. I am beaten

by all I ask for. I have no ear
for trite expressions. I know
her concern is my knowledge.

He sucks teeth. I am not enamoured
of his expression. It could be
that I am looking through my scream.

How It Is

I

Dippers, foggers, fatters, feeders, tubbers,
names lost and found, familiars that speak.
In the devil's hoils are Cradley's workers,
Robert Sherard enters. While Roger leaks
deathly green, they drink Burton's Return for ease.
Sherard notes the rot, the forfeit of teeth,
wages stopped for sewings, stalling, breeze.
He is over the wall in darkness to tea kettle broth,
Working Man's Beef – grand stuff in onions,
hymns for a living, The Lord Will Provide.
And the hangman's namesake – skeletons half done
by the salt-cake, mired children by their side.
Dog chain, cart chain, cow-ties, cables, graves.
They will not forge fetters for they are the slaves.

II

I open the pages and they vomit voices.
Words beggar compassion, grind the mind.
Women rock the baby while pounding chain,
the armless greet the legless in the Authors' Club.
Children work a rebellious treadle in some grotesque
fairground allegory, adding weight to the Oliver
not suited to women if over thirty-six pounds.
Small bodies swing on the lever: Children – join in.
They die in the mercy before one year of age.
So many still – Sierra Leone, Syria, the endless list.
The Primark label may be sewn in a fake garment
by one of conscience for Bangladesh workers.
I am just reading a book, my mind tired with testimony.
Sherard drags us into the mud of history.

Chainmakers: The Long Cry
Un long crie d'indignation retentit en ce moment[1]

It's the brewus I works in, out the back. Roar up heat,
fuel the furnace, forge dull links, beat blackened skin.
It roasts our innards, blasts our hot breath thin.

And the ring of it, the slam of the hammer, the clang
that cleaves my head at night, the red mist, the times
I'm reeling as the sun droops and the dark digs in.

Cradley's, Craigie Heath, Quarry Bank and Netherton.
Reece's down Maple Tree Lane. High Town is our rack –
we're Black Country, pounding pig iron, bloom and slack.

It's tricky work, chaining steel with our stringed hands,
wetting sweated backs. Watch for sparks as cut-offs fly,
birth the babby, back to work and wait for heat to die.

It's all spoil to us – we just makes our bread. Millie though
reaches a grimy hand to grab a spark, search the floor
for dull hot scrap. She won't make that mistake no more

not since I bound her up. It did heal, though she's the welt
to larn her, the chainmakers' fetter now she's not so thin.
White slaves we are. I put white lard on her weeping skin.

I tells her not to touch, not trip, not grip hot sparks, hot scrap,
not put it back 'til its cold, not fold a soft hand round rod iron,
sulking black. I says I'll leg-iron her if she don't pack it in.

We beat the little ones, the links. Paid by the hundred-weight,
it's just the way of it, that's what I say. Tuppence halfpenny
didn't help poor Lizzie, did it, when she passed away?

---

[1] 'A long cry of indignation is echoing today'; *L'Intransigeant*, (Paris, 1897).

Chainmakers: Hephaestus

The blackened God squats in his fire-box,
nostrils sharp with the reek of cinder and slag.
His molten eyes peer through set streams of lava.
He eases bent limbs in their clinker shell,
scrapes dull ash through his burnt bristle hair.

Soon the attendant will come, stir up his fierce belly,
set fire-fingers reaching heat through the outhouse,
scrape sharp nails through the pits and rust blast
of the anvil. The clang of the hammer will toll worship,
all must bow low at the altar of Mammon.

And here is the sacrifice – a soft daughter to feed him.
She peers in the crater, points fat fingers at his dark pupils,
waits for the hot brand to mark her golden skin.
She will be consumed. He waits for the acolyte mother.
Weeping fire-black, she escorts her little one in.

Chainmakers: Breaking Chains
Wednesday 19th October 1910: the strike is over.

Grainger's Lane Primitive: Mary Macarthur
spreads angel wings, tilts her megaphone
to the *Hammered Branch of the Chain Trade*,
to *Mrs C and her seven children working chain*,
there's *invidious distinction* in that. Pathé news
is filming, a lad – the age mine would have been –
turning the crank. We thought starvation would coffin us,
thought our cracked lungs would give out no shout.
Now *Rouse Ye Women* with a belly-full of bread
for our stopping, for our nine-week strike-back.
They say we're the guardians, bloody *guardians
of the inherent dignity of man*. We're the radicals
of Cradley, renegades in our own tough mills,
a woman chain forging a thousand links a day.
Think of Patience Round, an *aged striker of 79*;
think of Lizzie; think of Millie's little hand
what's saved her from working the hammers –
Mr Forsyte says she can go as a tween maid
up at the house if I'll let her. *Inn of Tranquillity*
that will be next to our rough midden –
she can wear a new hat. We've tuppence halfpenny
to trumpet and a rod of iron in our bellies.
We never thought it would come to that.

Cradley Manifesto

Do not go beg from them as belongs to me.
Our withered children must fill their mouths by right.
These burnt and blistered hands are not a plea –

our birth-pangs are the sweated toil you see.
As pale lead-lined skin cools with the night
do not go beg from them as belongs to me,

the years stripped from us are the daily fee.
We slave in brutal sun and in the fading light –
these burnt and blistered hands are not our plea.

There's not a woman born who envies me
the roasting of my skin, my fading sight,
yet I'll not beg from them as belongs to me.

So as we dream our children can be free
of all we suffer in our man-made plight,
these burnt and blistered hands are not a plea.

No – they demand a life, a guarantee
that soon we will be winners in our fight.
I will not beg from them as belongs to me –
these burnt and blistered hands are not my plea.

Emily

Here is thunder, the thud of hooves on turf,
the crowd's roar as the lash cracks my flanks
with pain a thousand times the stinging rain
on the gallops in Winter where we train.

Here is mud, myriad cuts in the hopeful grass
like sickle scars on the earth's skin.
I am the punter's run, the tragedy of odds,
the even chance of a nose-band's whisker
ahead of the game. I am for the King.

I lean the turn in the track, wracking withers,
stringy tendons' glide into the final gallop,
the ride of a lifetime with a clinging boy on top
like a Roman bronze to jockey my speed.

I catch a flash of purple and brown
that tangles my hooves for a moment
and I am soaring and plunging and rolling
and the whip hand is nothing and the ground
thuds my body like a giant fist wrenching fetters
and tendons screaming and the crowd is screaming
and it is over.

The boy is still. I lie still. She is a bunch of drab rags.
Still. And the crowd echoes – why Emily?
Why Emily?
Why?

Connie Markievicz

The countess stops in the doorway.
What plans and schemes are here
as pale light washes the raw planked floor.
She presses the heels of her button gloved hands
together, holds dust moted air like a lily.

Room for the easel by the window,
the dressing case to go upstairs.
She pulls a brown overall from the dun valise
then over her head with it to tab her two hips,
telling of just the one child and a silk kimono.

She steps through to the low back kitchen,
admires the stone larder slab, the bleached
wooden slats that frame the chipped sink.
The table bears a coarse blue jug, yellow-bright
with jonquils and small herbs of the season.

And a note, cream paper, a flourish of script –
Read these – they may be of interest. Pages curl.
She turns to bang a zinc kettle under the gush
of the tap, waits the carter to come from the back.
Words will rise, they will rise. They will rise.

A Binding

A binding, I am Abraham –
a woman's hands – the heave.
You raise the blade, you twist the knot –
and burn the ash of love.

A Moses basket – spears of rush –
the icy rime, the hoar.
The child smiles – a hand is reached –
and life is lived for more.

Deny the bond – and smear the seal –
cut lust and rub it raw.
The ram rears up – the thicket stopped –
and none has gone before.

Isaac pull the strands aside –
the air – the certain thought.
Yet lady blaze my troubled eyes –
for who can find the heart?

I put my cup on that high shelf

If I leaned just a little more
        over this banister, this shaky rail,

I might go tumbling down the stairs,
        a heavy rumble, a somersaulting free fall

into space. The crash, the mess! The weeping
        until the paramedics, pony-tailed, arrived

solicitous while they worked their haematic magic
        with pallid tubes and tragic spine boards –

all in vain. Then there would not be much merry chat.
        Actually I don't want that. I have my voice

my words, my time, I'm fine. But reaching for this cup
        defines the line, the tiny breath, the choice.

Nest Egg

All that hoarding and tucking in,
too big, too small, too snagged with little branches
taking off in their own direction.
Too much in any storm,
swaying with the eddies and currents that buffet
while tidying round the sticks that bind.

When pregnant, I would retch so loud.
Not nesting, but on my knees –
such uncouth postures. Only one thing
made the moss stick as I prepared the lining.

The cuckoo was what kept me happy,
yet levering it out these twenty years after
has not been hard.
I did not even hear it hit the ground.

Wolves

Windows are sharp and brittle things.
In our bungalow they are often open,
even at night when anyone could come.

Once my sister saw a curious face
in the opening, like a blueish full moon.
She jumped up to pull the curtains tight
and fled back to bed.

She did not tell my mother.

At night windows change.
In my dreams they melt away.
That's when the wolves come
slinking along the shadowed wall,
where the grass tufts are thin
in the gravel gully.

I know they are there by their breathing.
I have to keep quiet but they are there.
Soon their rough snouts will snuffle the opening,
dark shapes will flow over the window sill
into the blackness under my bed

where my childhood sleeps.

Saturday Morning

I am walking on the thin chalk turf
and the sun is lighting my pale legs.
I am to play out now 'til lunchtime
though no-one knows when that is.

The sun is lighting my pale legs.
I am hoping that my Dad will come
though no one knows when that is –
perhaps he will play crab rides with us.

I am hoping that my Dad will come,
bringing the Lambretta that broke his ribs.
Perhaps he will play crab rides with us
and he might carry more than one child.

He's bringing his Lambretta that broke his ribs
when it fell on the ice with him screaming under,
and he might carry more than one child.
Perhaps I will not fall down as it hits.

When it fell on the ice with him screaming under
they taped him round so he could not breathe.
Perhaps I will not fall down as it hits –
the worst was stripping the hairs on his chest.

They taped him round so he could not breathe
and we watched wide eyed from the bedroom door.
The worst was stripping the hairs on his chest
while Mother was thinking of buying a car.

We watched wide eyed from the bedroom door
but I am to play out now 'til lunchtime.
While Mother is thinking of buying a car
I am walking out to the thin chalk turf.

My Sister's Bones

They were a desiccated jumble
in a dry orange-box with pale slats
and a stencilled reference number.

Stringy fibrous coverings,
shrivelled osteocytes shrunk
in their lacunae, a trabecular web
tracking forces for a lifetime and beyond.
Long bones as yellow as the marrow
which once sustained them.

Our daily help thought they made a mess
of her tidy floor, were not very nice
for children to be playing with.

My sister's bones.

At night she would take some to bed,
a femur perhaps or flaring scapula,
caress the intersecting planes and grooves,
cartilage connections and smooth insertions
to see how they were fixed, where surfaces
would glide. Reading with her fingertips
an osseous world internalised.

She became the surgeon Father had hoped to be.
My father's bones – the ones he gave
my sister, and me.

Lycanthrope

This mud slick footpath, oily as sunk ships,
where the rigging trees are stark as a wreck
is where I walk my thoughts.

It is not a black shadow meatily thrusting
which dogs my steps, but a chimera hyena
with rough breath who prints my path
this English winter. He sinks his shoulders
to slink along the sharp barbed fence
that wires me in self-doubt.

I'm keeping safe inside the cage –
he's out, I'm in. Rough tan patches
scrofulate his flanks where all my hopes
were wearing thin.

So now I'm out on the bare line
where buttercups will burst before
their time. Sparse grass thrusts up ahead
ruffling the breeze. He's not seen.

Bramble thickets gestate sour fruit
beneath the shade, as unknown questions
protract their claws yet sheath their blades.

My Blue Tattoo

To me it is lampshade skin.
It is where it would begin.
It is my meat label,
my loss of control. It
has been done to me
against my will. I want
it not to be there still.

It sits just to the left
as I look down my chest,
off-kilter. It is very small
and navy blue. Not
of much consequence
the oncologist says.

It spreads a little now,
leaks into surrounding cells,
seeps dyestuff into winter
dermis. It does not ask
permission. Contaminated
pthalo blue; monastral blue.
It is not my blue. I do not
want it there. I do not want

all it means to have it there –
I had that time. I am here,
yet it is still here
on my chest.

Searching the Lost

I am toiling up the long hill.
My satchel bumps my back, my legs tired
from the hated trudge to the hockey ground.
Perhaps Rosie will bring new bread to tear
crusted, spread with Granny's rich jam –
raspberry or gooseberry, both good.

I am lying hard on the floor, a sticky
sleeping bag around my legs. Beside me
on the raised bed, my child struggles
to breathe. That time – that moment –
do we call the doctor, run for the door?
I touch the steaming bowl between us,
drop the viscous crystals in.
What shall we do? he says.

I am walking the circle of the garden.
The roses bear sugared names.
I am thinking of the day ahead –
the daily crucifixion, the Calvary
of us all in the hospital basement.
Now there is no room for sweet air,
no room on the benches for two
in the ring. Just a little solace.

Stocks

You have driven me down to the sins of women,
forced my feet into bedrock of the earth.

I did not steal a turnip, nor even a look,
though I may have whistled to myself.

I know my mind. It takes my sinews through
these rough hoops into the rub of an open sore.

Folk here like compliance in domesticity.
I may have left a candle burning in the small east window

while I wrote at night. It may have sent signals.
I gaze at the iron leg clamps, hinged at either end,

the central locking pin in lead. I wonder
who will pair me up? Sheep are easier to tup

than strong women bred in this red mud.

My Mistress Masters All
In response to William Shakespeare's Sonnet 130

Well! I have task to take with all you say:
my lips are reddened by the best of blush,
my breasts mine to express, or gladly play
with as I choose; they are the royal flush
to use for work or show. I coolly smoke
my cigarettes, drink whisky sours – I raise
a curving finger to the false and stoke
my smouldering rays. And so I nightly praise
my sisters all. I love their schemes, the smiles
we joust with all our men. Our laughter stays
with us to underpin our thoughts and wiles.
We link our arms to stride the parting ways.
We walk the ground with firmest foot and hand
and choose to love: we know just where we stand.

Choice

It's not a big deal which way to take.
I did pause – the mile or so of tarmac, occasional cars,
or the rocky track past forgotten dells and fields
and woods backed by the wall of fells. Still snow.
There could be early primroses despite the ice
on puddles, cobbles levered loose from fields,
catkins lambent against the sky, a flash of chaffinch.
Long tailed tits might swing the fragile birch twigs,
twitter in the morning breeze.
So that's my way.

Even from far off, he is not a walker.
He swaggers, a gap between his legs. Jeans not fit.
Something about his black anorak as he draws closer –
greasy, slightly torn. A thrust. The look he gives.
I am calculating options but there are none.
The stony winter fields deep in mud
are not a place to run. So much wrong.
I see the caravan, pigeon dropped,
plastic windows cracked, a grimy curtain.
And a frosted four-by-four abandoned
steeply up the hill. I wish so hard
I hadn't worn my much-loved tweedy skirt,
the one with pheasants embroidered in so many shades,
dark tights, brown boots. I want thick walking trousers,
over-trousers as a suit of armour and a stick perhaps
if I could use it. It hangs between us. He leers his lip,
hitches another swagger in his gait. I can feel his weight.
He comes towards me, fingers closing round my neck
in my mind's eye – three reddened marks seen later
in the first report. I could turn back, but that means walking
just in front of him. He drawls a challenge. I look fierce
as I know how, curse my damned skirt, brush past and stride
so fast while knowing if he turns I can't beat his loose limbs.

My breathing's broken only by my thudding feet –
faster, faster but don't run, don't give yourself away,
concentrate on distance, forcing out a space between us,
reeling in the village turn, the glimpse of smoke rising lazy
in the silent air. Still I'm listening to see if he is there.
I have a force field in my ears. I even risk a look.
One more deep bend to climb up sandstone sills
that weep moisture even at the height of sun.
Strap ferns sprout in crevices of tumbled walls.
Sheep bones lie – some are lichened, strong.
They say that murdered women put up a fight.
It's not a big deal which way to take.

Zebra Longwing

Sunlight tips the disc of table, the emptied cup,
    the smear of jam. I tear open your card and sit

to feel a sense of airy flutter against my hand,
    the disconnect of fractured breeze.

A vibration of not really feet, the tenuous touching
    of soft yellow, a creamy petal edge

above the determined fractal swell of buds fading
    to grey shade. The mesh.

And the astonishing stripes, the white,
    the power of black to soar. Four scarlet beads.

Your writing stutters from all the medication,
    the raw years of not knowing.

Peeling the stamp, the walk to posting. The brutal choosing
    of this morning.

Walk in the Wood

I am the badger draining the sett, two slabs,
white meat of grey stone split by scraping,

the trough of a broken pipe-lip roughed out
by worn words whiling away darkness, a lichen-sink

concealing a name. I am dark trunks facing north
and south, neither slime nor suede-head baby fungus,

erupting hand-backs that mortify the earth.
I am not neat and nurture, I am the strange feeling

stepping up this grass, the start of questions,
the uncertainty of sharp smoke, the tang of lead

in the twisted bucket, the sharp lack of leather, the skip
of a deer scut, a reddened kite in the deer lick.

There is darkness in these seven trees made of their own
 shade. There is pale precarious leaf-fall

with each stirring, a stray laurel shifts its leaf-gloss,
the twisted black of yew in straight lines,

soft milled earth nosed by mole snouts,
fullered to leaving, dull sheen on brickwork

where winter's back has rubbed, grey slates
shouldering leaf-mould. Verdigris leaks as I click

the gate shut, thoughts still touched
by the bucket's mark.

Part Speech
*Since I have cast my lot, please golden-crowned Aphrodite,
let me win this round!* Sappho, c 630 – c 570 BC

The sound of hot wheat opening
hushes birdsong.

The crocodile yawns,
spewing rats of rot, tight knots.

Wasps masticate words,
glue sets our options

like a left hook
for a dumb fish plated.

Crusts of armour
cod our piece of work –

mud fish lurking.
Shadows take our lungs

like ideas ripped
to tear their meanings out.

Stripped from womankind,
the peeled sap-juiced bark,

the girl-child is the withy.

Tooth Fairy

One for the hand bell ringers
at eighteen pence a ton.

Two for the cast-offs in the work-house
when we're done.

Three for the salt cake and the liquids of death
we breathe as we're slaving to eventual rest.

Four for the gruel we stir in the can, the crusts
for the rats back where they began.

Five for the oiling of lime-slaked skin
we wipe with paper before we go home.

Six for the muzzle we wear in the heat,
seven for the brandy they give us too late.

Eight for the turning that lays us to rest,
nine for the nitre bag wrapping our legs.

But none for the tooth fairy. Easy they fade
in chloride and vitriol, leaving us pegs

that won't need the puller. No teeth
for the pillow. No pillow for a sinner.

Le Grand Art de ne Pas Tout Dire[2]

They likes to be there when there's
something going, when Father chucks them
a bit of bread. It's past ten o'night at the old
slipper maker's, with his well-fed
happy children, who likes to be there.

> *I snooze when I can*
> *when my belly's aching.*
> *It stills when I'm dozing*
> *then Fether comes in.*

>> The proof de visit of the accuracy
>> of statements is the stones and feathers,
>> wires, fragments of cork in the layers,
>> making the great knives' breaking
>> a likely event.

We shares the bed,
'tis a little stained pallet.

It's falsehood and slander and gross
traduction, and all for describing
a little stained bed. The fictitious case
for false protection, such inaccurate
statements of alleged pauper labour,
when as all acknowledge

> *we likes to be there.*

>> Being true pictures of Certain
>> Social Conditions in the Kingdom

---

[2] *The great art of not telling everything.*

> Yet the White Slaves of England
> are given bona fides, for the Leeds
> tailor operatives are well paid
> as a body, most cheerful
> in appearance.

And we rouse ourselves night time
to catch what scraps from the table
as we is able to scrabble
with our little dull fingers.

And they treat it as nothing 'cept
adulteration of fabrics. Even
tailoresses in Leeds Punishing Houses
are hard-working and willing.
For as all will acknowledge

> *we likes to be there.*

These are houses of great sanitary principle,
> with no public awareness of any exception.

>> Backbones of trade are the fabric
>> manufactories. More libels refuted
>> are the true Hymn of England,
>> at the Gates and Pillars of the great
>> Clothing Trade.

Skywatching in Yosemite

Our hands splay out to spread the turf,
fingers digging in the musty dirt
like muscular mudbank clams.
Our backs and butts press down
flat out among the Sneezeweed,
grid-lined by the Merced.
Rock arches loop high to scoop
the pitchy velvet. Phosphorescence
picks out the Falls beyond the pines,
stark branches dissect starry swathes.
Each constellation pricks our eyes.
Astonishing patterns fade and flow
around the glittering granite rim,
the soft slash of Milky Way pulls us in.
This is us five as we will never be again –
laid out like spoons, touching hands
on mountain meadows, watching for bears
and the possibilities of shooting stars.

America

Smooth your finger tips
    along the neat stock. Admire
        the crisp click as the spring-loader

locks. Feel the machined lip
    on the chunk of the grip –
        how it fits strong in the grasp

of the hand. Keep us safe, Jeb!
    Keep us safe. Now your name's on the block
        we know how to lock down our neighbours,

take action on fright. It's the heart of the gun, see,
    the knock-down at night. Take off the trigger guard
        as we settle in snug. Hit the guts of our dreams

with the boys in the shade who took lead to get laid –
    thirty-three thousand this year alone,
        mothered in grief. We saw them, they're gone.

Keep us safe Jeb, keep us safe, while the rest of the world
    slumps with broadsheets and tea cups and unmanly words.
        It's the gun in the mind which is loaded and primed.

My Wall

My wall will be beautiful.
Pale flowers will drift across the stone,
creepers will trail soft tendrils
with downy-backed leaves like hands

reaching out on both its sides. Birds
will nest in the tangle of new growth.
They will sing in that tentative way
birds have as they emerge in Spring.

There will be many gates. None
will be locked. There will be no Arbeit arch.
It will be understood that each is free,
that each gate will always stand open.

My wall will have kind custodians
to tend tired travellers as they arrive.
Like Mediaeval monks, they will wash feet,
bathe hands, make up simple truckle beds.

Each family can stay together, take time
for the very old to live, to pass away
while the birds are singing. We can all
mourn by our accepted practices.

There will be many grassy places
brightening the grey base stones.
Here the children will play together
and this is what will protect us.

Washington Seashore

They move fast, these men.
They are the standing wave
we must disrupt with our levees.
They are the ones who are frightened,
surfing the spittle of fear.
They like their women draped
empty on the wet reef.

Like breakers, they batter
the basalt shore, burst sharp clefts
with an injured fist, detonating
stone-fall in the slave-wrought mine.
Their mouths are the glint-grit
of quartz grains in rough rock
fractured by frost which chisels
their hard cheeks. They do not smile.

Their waves of resentment
have no natural swell to ebb
and flow their feelings.
They are the baked rind
of a bleached rubber tyre
stuck hard in hot sand.
They are the snatch of chaotic current
that may drag a body at any time.
And they like it that way.

Newcastle Down

The truncated clip of a colleague's feet.
The speed that I walk back to my room,
tilted sideways by a heavy rucksack
away from sharp looks.

Sitting on sunlit grass, eating cherries
in my own time.

Seagull shrieks in calm rooms.
The repeated scrape of a tethered dog
like a damp rag rubbed hard on a dusted board.

Synchronous cyclists, their streamlined helmets
like matching halves of a ribbed black clam.

Salted fish wedged in cracked paving,
hard sinews of dirt-stained fingers
wrenching stringy flesh from sparse bones
to feed thin children.

The determined cheerfulness of women
peddling cheap shoes in large shops.

Lord Grey, franchising the common man
from the top of his limestone column.
Women, of course, cannot vote.

The steep fall of cobbles towards port quays,
figured plaster on a jettied wall.

Ghost ships still berth from the Baltic,
their sailors leaning to pull on a pipe.

The curve of stone, sweeping the street down
to the source of riches below Graingertown,

the sweet faecal reek of the Tyne.

Zazel attempts to become the first human cannonball
1877, the Royal Aquarium, London

Now I've gone and done it, stuck in the barrel, ramrod straight,
best not to think, all too late. Fired up and ready to go alright.
Balmy on the crumpet, like it or lump it, this is how it goes:

I stands neat, feet on the pad, *Knees tight, pretend you're a lad.*
Meaning what I'd like to know – fine for 'im to go *one, two,
three* then watch the show, a gal-sneaker at the big bengo.

Mr Farini – he's alright. He's had me since I were a nipper,
though more's on the cards he says, all chipper. Anyway,
he lights the brand, touches a lever behind the stand.

Then *One* he says, *Yes Mr Farini, Two* he says, *Yes Mr Farini,
Three* he says, the crowd says *Ooh* and I'm there with a bang,
soaring through them fish tanks, no batty fang,

like a razor-clam tossed to me brother, bored cod the left of me,
to the right another – a shoal of mack'rel, all clemmed up.
And just when I'm losing touch, I'll flip me feet,

somersault over, nice and neat. Tickety boo I'm floating down,
me jelly fish skirt like a muslin crown, thick flesh tights
to keep a girl tidy, sequins flash on me satin pridey.

Sweet Mary on the terrace from sea to land –
Little Archie, take me hand. So Mum I didn't mean it,
Dad where've you been? Billy Boy why'd you do it?

What you laughing at yer bum and baccas? Takes a princess
to get this right. So it's *One* says *Farini, Two* says *Farini,
Three* says *Farini* and I'm off up the night.

On Shingle Beach

Sea sweeps, sucks
        exact. Crunch two

marbled. Ingrained sea
        suck. Sweeps

Footfall, landfall, falling
        with. Tide. Tidefall

backpull. Hair back, back pack,
        standing. Just standing.

Bladder snap, wrack-black sea slack
        stone speck. Stones crack

light. Light sight, night sight. Flight
        in seagrains. Seastar. Sea

line, far lone. Out to
        sea lanes, sea lines. Water

shine. Swoosh. Push pebbles
        creak feet touch. Foam

webs caul fat. Flat fat. Light fat. Light
        tower. Past placed. Spaced

time suck. Wet suck shining,
        grey grains shining

wind star, turbine tower, blade power
        ship back. Back flat. Flat line,

eyes shine. Back flat shiplap. Bone
        salt. Salt bones, sea groans,

sweeps. Suck. Stick stuck
        sea bones. Lost in stone chat.

Night-time in Brexit

So here's the dream: silvered beads of rain
rake serried spears down shining grass,
the gracious sweeps of briar rose, the steeps.
A hare loops out from the angled bank,
staples the roadway in quivers as it lopes,
flares left and right to jink through a gateway
and is gone. We are travelling on.

The faces of the actors float pale against
the gloom. Oberon is stately in his silver robe,
Titania stretches sated limbs, she feels despoiled.
Peter gives his sturdy piece, clasps pasty arms together,
kneads his hands. From where he stands
all will be well – as far as he can tell this play
is amplified, is not within. So we can all begin.

Now Puck dips his stems in vexing juice of dew,
plants his heel to vaporize the elements we thought
we knew. And as the poison bites it cuts us through
as random love is wont to do – and leaves us wondering
just who is panting now inside the ass's head.
Who weaves the threads to twitch his clouded web?
Perhaps it is the warhorse snorting there instead.

Now here's the thing. As Bottom lonely stands
to take his bow, he strokes a hand along his sodden dress,
drags the clinging fabric anyhow. He rubs crusted dust
from fleecy eyes, pulls Pyramus from the fractured wall,
stands tiptoe while sloven Thisbe sleeps.
Behind the stage, wet with a shower of golden stars
and slurried mud from sodden boots, Titania weeps.

Burns Night

I have supped and I've tupped on your trust Jean, trust,
on the neeps and the tatties from the dust, just dust.
I've taken what is mine as I must, as I must –
you're a good wee girl so I thrust thrust thrust.
The childer all bewilder in their shrieking shrouds
and your cries were the fainter for theirs were so loud.
And you rocked by the lock as I thrust, as I thrust
and I took what was mine in the dust dust dust.
So be raising of your glass to take your fill slow fill,
you'll be thinking of your bairnies when they're still so still.
To the rocking and the locking as we flew flew flew,
with the thunder of the scalade that was midnight blue.
For I took what was mine in the glory of the night
and I leave to our parting, the wrong from the right.

Blood

Mother, did you tell me? Certainly
not of sex. I worked that out
in various combinations,
learnt to dissect lust from love.
So, Mother, did you tell me?
I leaned over my aching belly,
a dullness low on my bones,
the dread of strings and sodden lint
between my legs. One ruined day
was cut from me like a black stone
melted deep in its own hole
high on Ben Nevis in pristine snow.
Saved by thick tweed, men's
woollen underwear worn for warmth
soaked up the clots until the refuge
of a crowded hut.

And then I was delivered,
floated down on wings of whispered fire,
a ripcord that bore me up.
Not to be used the first time –
in case of what? It might get stuck
up there, destroy the virgin urge
to try our luck. But we were laughing,
jingling change, walking high
in tights and rolled up skirts.
So Mother – what more could you say?
We were tampon girls with money to burn
and on our way.

Woke

And you, they say? Always there is the taint
of wasting, a sense of gap,
something missing from the daily chain.
It could be seen almost as a strength –
the years of afterschool, birthday cards, so little power
to challenge power, far from the thoughts that woke

me to motherhood as unshackled blessing. I am woke
to knowing that small hands have waved off that taint
and thrown it out, squeezed out the power
to press it hard on glass, press out the gap
of hands, turn it over with their strength
to become links, and link the chain

to something strong. Take hold to grasp that rough chain
that's half perceived, a voice – not listened to – that woke
to skin, to veins, to tendons stretched to tension, to strength
released from freedom by freedom, the choice to reject the taint
of faint heart lost, to adventure without knowing. A gap
between unyielding surface and its bloodless power.

And it is a rough game, this power
to banish women from the network chain,
the not speaking about what is, the gap
within the heart of substance, awoke
to distance, the snarl of taint,
the feint to dodge the strength

that comes by right, entitlement. The strength
that avoids how women hide their power –
the glance away, the scanning taint
of frank disdain, the human chain
broken by what matters. The eye awoke
to all that's missing, the common stinking gap

as women bridge the gap
by little things, by tattle, serving as a strength
the very system by which we're broke. Yet we are woke
to this, to treachery, to trappings of the power
we see through, the bite of years that binds us round, the chain
of questions stifled. It's the not asked which gives the taint

if only we can unfurl that gap, seize hold of power
by saying yes we will, today, the strength of being in the chain
of women woke, that says – so what – we like that taint.

Blue Bed Women

Five stones heavy on our head and hands,
climbing ladders to stack up the tan.
Five stones scraping the bloom and silver,
bleeding sweat from the edge of the muzzle,
taunting shadows in the bed of our nails.

We are the blueys, susceptible when young.
The things that are done here are not
for the other. Wall-eyed, cock-eyed,
we are walled in the stack-yards, endangered
by dividends, colic and pains.

Thirteen weeks for the fumes to finish,
longer than the babies in our tainted wombs.
Lost seven, lost two – sickly is all. Exhaustion
a mercy. Stripped of our teeth, moulded cold,
plumb-lined with poison and pocketed coins.

Wraiths of the lakes, we are silvered slatterns,
vapoured witless by the coming dark.

White Bed Women

Goose down, swan's down, antique cotton,
indah cotton, elin cotton, soft touch pillows,
perfectly smooth.

Blood red, menstrual red,
miscarriage red. Five children lost
while working the lead.

Brown bed, shared bed. Statemented
at Tyne Lead, date started, date
finished. One child born alive.

Weak women rejected. Must
fill the stomach prior. Difficulty
in doing away with females.

More susceptible. Not susceptible.
All males on heavy work. They feels
the hoars – it drains their fresh colour.

Thirteen weeks to strip the white bed.
You there – Go get your muzzle.
It works the joints, twists the arms.

Wrist-drop common. Her Majesty's
Inspectorate. Headache. Convulsion
extremely fatal. Three days only

to a Work House death-bed, with
The Day Thou Gavest. Billowing pillows
boiled to cleanliness, perfectly smooth.

Eidólons

Here they come, the eidólons
arisen from rough words. Expect
spectres, spirits, apparitions,
pale phantoms manifesting.

But speak softly, for they hear us.
Stroke gently, for their hair is sensual.
Lifted lips can sip at meanings
along with gruel from a feeder spout.

Beside us are their unborn children
bouncing knees to try their walking.
I will take them to the sand strand,
help them splash hands in the water.

And lying there, a leather muzzle
swollen stiff with tears and salt-crust;
dusted with the death it's dealing,
cast off by Home Secretary's Order.

Yes here they come, the eidólons,
the *pale, thin, insubstantial persons*.
And we are reaching through the ether,
joining hands to witness our existence.

Siren Sewn

I want to knit my fingers into these pale scars,
sink sharp nails into the edge of slack pleats.
Bite stray ends of cotton with the grind of my teeth
like the surgical sutures I bit off after my procedure.
My unwise mind told me the loops would catch,
that snipping them short would somehow circumvent
the reality of my asymmetry. The surgeon was male, kind.
He laughed. It is not a full mastectomy.

I want to probe this pale belly, I want urgently to unpick
these cotton stitches, their inexactitude, their frail starring
of the swell of torso, the touch of hips and clitoris below.
I want to press my hand gently down the lower folds
where thighs begin, feel the strength of a lengthening stride.
I want to unpeck the connection between sex and that raven neck.
I want to cry away the twine that seals the forbidden stretch.
I want to be uncut.

I want to unwind the beads that bind the cry of freedom
in that sharp raven's head. I want to forget the cruel tilt of beak,
the beady eye watching women as they dare to speak.
I want to lie. To sooth taut shoulders, run a smoothing hand
down a curve of back. Take back the harm to that brittle neck
elongated by its pitch-black beading. Strike off the shackles
preventing healing, preventing speech. I want to listen
to each stitch say its piece.

The Place at the Other Side

I think I may lie stateless a while on these calm
marble floors, stretch cracked hands up
towards the air. I will open the morning mortuary
with its slick milled doors, slide out my thoughts.
I have come to cool my lungs with unsayable things,
write them on the inside of my skin. I have hinges
in my thinking. I am separated by plate glass.

I will reach out to slip inside your oxidation,
feel the texture of that dark meat, rough out
those concavities. I think you know –
your mouth pouts that. You are bisected
by rough scars, scaled by the unrealistic anatomy
you inhabit. It must feel vulnerable to be so exposed.
You may be trying to climb inside my skin.

I observe your flesh as fetish; you enjoy that
as display. Your smooth skull excludes.
You disown the discs of your creviced chest,
suckle nothing but golden verdigris.
We could talk but I cannot hear what your lips
may spit. You master the tenets of your territory.
I am on the outside, trespassing its limits.

Indigo Dreams Publishing Ltd
24, Forest Houses
Cookworthy Moor
Halwill
Beaworthy
Devon
EX21 5UU
www.indigodreams.co.uk